This bible promise book was designed to help you successfully navigate through each area of your life. It's compiled of 58 topics that will help you significantly grow in God's word if you apply these scriptures on a daily basis. Allow God's promises to strengthen YOU and cause you to experience your best life!

Enjoy!

pro·mise

'präməs/

noun

- a declaration or assurance that one will do a particular thing or that a particular thing will happen.

- word (of honor), assurance, pledge, vow, guarantee, oath, bond, undertaking, agreement, commitment, contract, covenant

- an indication that something specified is expected or likely to occur.

- assure someone that one will definitely do, give, or arrange something; undertake or declare that something will happen.

- give one's word, swear, pledge, vow, undertake, guarantee, contract, engage, give an assurance

- give good grounds for expecting (a particular occurrence or situation)

- lead one to expect, point to, denote, signify, be a sign of, be evidence of, give hope of

Table of Contents

Abundance	10
Answered Prayers	12
Assurance	14
Blessing	16
Comfort	18
Compassion	20
Confidence	22
Courage	24
Decisions	26
Discernment	28
Encouragement	30
Eternal Life	32
Faith	34
Favor	36
God is Faithful	38
Focus	42
Forgiveness	44
Free from Fear	46
Freedom	48
Future	50
Giving	52
God's Goodness	54
Healing	56
Housing	60
Identity	62
Increase	64
Joy	66
Life	68
Long Life	70
Mercy	74

Table of Contents

Obedience	76
Patience	78
Peace	80
Perseverance	82
Plans	84
Prayer	86
Protection	88
Provision of God	92
Purpose	94
Reward	96
Righteousness	98
Seeking God	100
Self-Control	102
Sowing and Reaping	104
Stability	106
Strength	108
Success in Business	110
Thankfulness	112
Thoughts	114
In Times of Trouble	116
Trust	118
Understanding	120
Unity	122
Victory	124
Will of God	128
Wisdom	130
Work	134
Daily Affirmation	136
Prayer of Salvation	138

Who is this book for and how can it be used?

- **Evangelism tool** - It serves as a great tool for new believers. You may meet another guy that truly needs to be poured into and what better way than to give him a bible promise book so that as he starts his walk with Christ, he can grow spiritually

- **Personal Worship** - your bible promise book is a perfect companion to go along with your daily bible reading and devotion time

- **Men's Bible Study** - this serves as a great tool to use for your men's group and explore scriptures in 58 categories so that your group can memorize scriptures from the readings

- **Resource for Counselors** - this bible promise book serves as an excellent resource for counselors that need concise, easy to ready and easy to digest scriptures that they can pass along to those being counseled

This

bible promise book

belongs to:

_____

and was a *gift* from:

_____

Just our way of saying

thanks

for buying this book, we want
to give our readers a
FREE GIFT.

Email us at
biblepromisebooks@gmail.com

Title the email,
"MEN'S FREE E-GIFT" and we'll
send you a link to our
FREE E-book,
"7 Keys To Change Your Thinking"
as our way of saying,
you're awesome.

ABUNDANCE

an overflowing fullness; ample sufficiency; great plenty; more than enough; copious supply; superfluity; wealth

Thank You Father for supplying my life with great abundance in Jesus name. Amen.

Psalm 65:11

You crown the year with your bounty, and your carts overflow with abundance.

Philippians 4:19

And my God will meet all your needs according to the riches of his glory in Christ Jesus

2 Corinthians 9:8

And God is able to bless you abundantly, so that in all things at all times, having all that you need, you will abound in every good work.

Deuteronomy 28:12-13

The Lord will open the heavens, the storehouse of his bounty, to send rain on your land in season and to bless all the work of your hands. You will lend to many nations but will borrow from none. The Lord will make you the head, not the tail.

ABUNDANCE

ANSWERED PRAYERS

fulfilled, solved, or accomplished requests or petitions to God

Father, You said that if I ask anything according to Your will, You would do it. Thank You for answering my prayers. In Jesus name. Amen.

Proverbs 15:29
The Lord is far from the wicked, but he hears the prayer of the righteous.

Psalm 6:9
The Lord has heard my cry for mercy; the Lord accepts my prayer.

I John 5:14-16
This is the confidence we have in approaching God: that if we ask anything according to his will, he hears us. And if we know that he hears us —whatever we ask—we know that we have what we asked of him.

John 15:7
"If you remain in me, and my words remain in you, ask whatever you wish, and it will be done for you."

Psalm 66:19
But truly God has listened; he has attended to the voice of my prayer.

Matthew 7:7
Ask, and it will be given to you; seek, and you will find; knock, and it will be opened to you.

ANSWERED PRAYERS

ASSURANCE

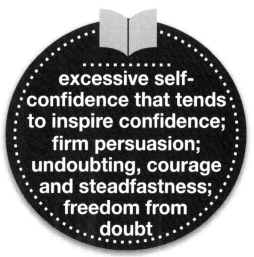

excessive self-confidence that tends to inspire confidence; firm persuasion; undoubting, courage and steadfastness; freedom from doubt

Father, I thank You for building my confidence and assurance in Your word, all the days of my life. In Jesus name. Amen.

Hebrews 11:1
Now faith is confidence in what we hope for and assurance about what we do not see.

1 Timothy 3:13
Those who have served well gain an excellent standing and great assurance in their faith in Christ Jesus.

Hebrews 10:22
Let us draw near to God with a sincere heart and with the full assurance that faith brings, having our hearts sprinkled to cleanse us from a guilty conscience and having our bodies washed with pure water.

Ephesians 3:12
In him and through faith in him we may approach God with freedom and confidence.

1 John 5:15
And if we know that he hears us—whatever we ask—we know that we have what we asked of him.

ASSURANCE

BLESSING

the empowerment to prosper and have success; God's enablement on your life; the power of elevation

Father I thank You for the blessing on my life that empowers me in every area of my life. In Jesus name.

Psalm 21:3
You came to greet him with rich blessings and placed a crown of pure gold on his head.

Psalm 128:2
You will eat the fruit of your labor; blessings and prosperity will be yours.

Proverbs 10:22
The blessing of the Lord brings wealth, without painful toil for it.

Jeremiah 17:7
But blessed is the one who trusts in the Lord, whose confidence is in him

Deuteronomy 28:8
The Lord will send a blessing on your barns and on everything you put your hand to. The Lord your God will bless you in the land he is giving you.

Deuteronomy 28:2
All these blessings will come on you and accompany you if you obey the Lord your God

BLESSING

COMFORT

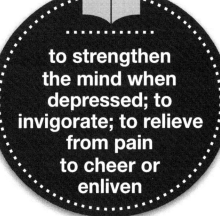

to strengthen
the mind when
depressed; to
invigorate; to relieve
from pain
to cheer or
enliven

Father, I thank You for Your word
always bringing comfort to me
when I need it most.
In Jesus name. Amen.

2 Corinthians 1:4
Who comforts us in all our troubles, so that we can comfort those in any trouble with the comfort we ourselves receive from God.

Isaiah 61:2
To proclaim the year of the Lord's favor and the day of vengeance of our God, to comfort all who mourn

Philippians 4:7
And the peace of God, which transcends all understanding, will guard your hearts and your minds in Christ Jesus.

Psalm 55:22
Cast your cares on the Lord and He will sustain you; he will never let the righteous fall.

Matthew 11:28
Come to me, all you who are weary and burdened, and I will give you rest.

COMFORT

COMPASSION

mixed passion, and love that arises when you are confronted with another's suffering and feel motivated to alleviate that suffering

Father, I thank You for always having compassion for me and always alleviating my suffering. In Jesus name. Amen.

Psalm 116:5
The Lord is gracious and righteous; our God is full of compassion.

Psalm 102:13
You will arise and have compassion on Zion, for it is time to show favor to her; the appointed time has come.

Psalm 103:4
Who redeems your life from the pit and crowns you with love and compassion

Colossians 3:12
Therefore, as God's chosen people, holy and dearly loved, clothe your-selves with compassion, kindness, humility, gentleness and patience.

Isaiah 30:18
Yet the Lord longs to be gracious to you; therefore he will rise up to show you compassion. For the Lord is a God of justice. Blessed are all who wait for him!

COMPASSION

CONFIDENCE

full trust, faith & reliance; belief in the total dependency or trustworthiness in the reliability of a person or thing

Father, In the name of Jesus,
I thank You for building my confidence
in the promises of Your word. Amen.

Hebrews 10:35

So do not throw away your confidence; it will be richly rewarded.

Hebrews 4:16

Let us then approach God's throne of grace with confidence, so that we may receive mercy and find grace to help us in our time of need.

1 John 5:14

This is the confidence we have in approaching God: that if we ask anything according to his will, he hears us.

Phillipians 4:13

I can do all this through him who gives me strength.

Proverbs 3:26

For the Lord will be at your side and will keep your foot from being snared.

Jeremiah 17:7

But blessed is the one who trusts in the Lord, whose confidence is in him.

CONFIDENCE

COURAGE

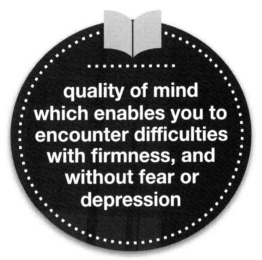

quality of mind which enables you to encounter difficulties with firmness, and without fear or depression

Thank You Father for giving me the courage I need to live a victorious life. In Jesus name.
Amen.

Joshua 1:7
Be strong and very courageous. Be careful to obey all the law my servant Moses gave you; do not turn from it to the right or to the left, that you may be successful wherever you go.

Joshua 1:9
Have I not commanded you? Be strong and courageous. Do not be afraid; do not be discouraged, for the Lord your God will be with you wherever you go.

Philippians 1:20
I eagerly expect and hope that I will in no way be ashamed, but will have sufficient courage so that now as always Christ will be exalted in my body, whether by life or by death.

Deuteronomy 31:6
Be strong and courageous. Do not be afraid or terrified because of them, for the Lord your God goes with you; he will never leave you nor forsake you.

COURAGE

DISCERNMENT

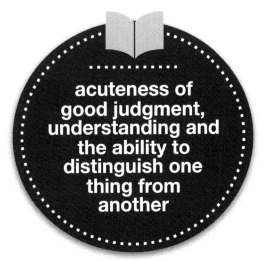

acuteness of good judgment, understanding and the ability to distinguish one thing from another

Father, I thank You that I exercise great judgement and the spirit of discernment concerning every decision. In Jesus name. Amen.

Psalm 119:125

I am your servant; give me discernment that I may understand your statutes.

Proverbs 28:2

When a country is rebellious, it has many rulers, but a ruler with discernment and knowledge maintains order.

Proverbs 16:21

The wise in heart are called discerning, and gracious words promote instruction.

Philippians 1:9-10

And this is my prayer: that your love may abound more and more in knowledge and depth of insight, so that you may be able to discern what is best and may be pure and blameless for the day of Christ

James 1:5

If any of you lacks wisdom, you should ask God, who gives generously to all without finding fault, and it will be given to you

DISCERNMENT

ENCOURAGEMENT

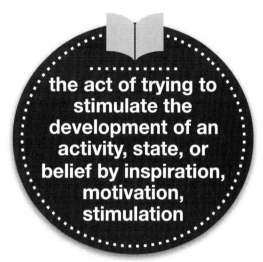

the act of trying to stimulate the development of an activity, state, or belief by inspiration, motivation, stimulation

Father, I thank You for teaching me how to encourage myself in the Lord and for using me to be an encouragement to others. In Jesus name.

Romans 15:5
May the God who gives endurance and encouragement give you the same attitude of mind toward each other that Christ Jesus had

2 Thessalonians 2:16
May our Lord Jesus Christ himself and God our Father, who loved us and by his grace gave us eternal encouragement and good hope

Psalm 10:17
You, Lord, hear the desire of the afflicted; you encourage them, and you listen to their cry

Isaiah 40:31
But those who hope in the Lord will renew their strength. They will soar on wings like eagles; they will run and not grow weary, they will walk and not be faint.

1 Thessalonians 5:11
Therefore encourage one another and build each other up, just as in fact you are doing.

ENCOURAGEMENT

ETERNAL LIFE

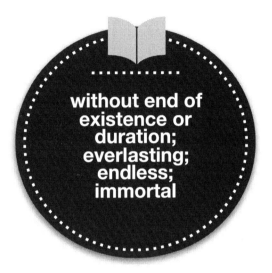

**without end of
existence or
duration;
everlasting;
endless;
immortal**

*Father, I thank You for the promise
of Eternal Life. In Jesus name.
Amen.*

1 John 2:17

The world and its desires pass away, but whoever does the will of God lives forever.

Romans 6:23

For the wages of sin is death, but the gift of God is eternal life in Christ Jesus our Lord.

John 3:36

Whoever believes in the Son has eternal life, but whoever rejects the Son will not see life, for God's wrath remains on them.

John 10:27-29

My sheep listen to my voice; I know them, and they follow me. I give them eternal life, and they shall never perish; no one will snatch them out of my hand. My Father, who has given them to me, is greater than all; no one can snatch them out of my Father's hand.

ETERNAL LIFE

FAITH

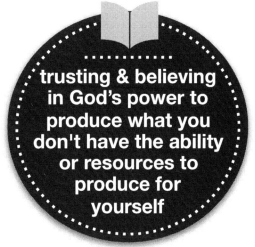

trusting & believing in God's power to produce what you don't have the ability or resources to produce for yourself

Thank You Father God for giving me the measure of faith to be fully persuaded of Your promises. In Jesus name. Amen.

1 Corinthians 16:13

Be on your guard; stand firm in the faith; be men of courage; be strong

Hebrews 11:6

And without faith it is impossible to please God, because anyone who comes to him must believe that he exists and that he rewards those who earnestly seek him

Romans 1:17

For in the gospel the righteousness of God is revealed—a righteousness that is by faith from first to last, just as it is written: The righteous will live by faith.

2 Corinthians 5:7

For we live by faith, not by sight.

Hebrews 11:1

Now faith is confidence in what we hope for and assurance about what we do not see.

FAITH

FAVOR

kindness done or granted; any act of grace; Advantage; to afford advantages for success; to aid

*Thank You Father God for Your favor
surrounding me like a shield,
all the days of my life.
In Jesus name.*

Psalm 5:12

Surely, Lord, you bless the righteous; you surround them with your favor as with a shield.

Numbers 6:25-26

The Lord make his face shine on you and be gracious to you; the Lord turn his face toward you and give you peace.

Psalm 102:13

You will arise and have compassion on Zion, for it is time to show favor to her; the appointed time has come.

Psalm 90:17

May the favor of the Lord our God rest on us; establish the work of our hands for us— yes, establish the work of our hands.

Psalm 84:11

For the Lord God is a sun and shield; the Lord bestows favor and honor; no good thing does he withhold from those whose walk is blameless.

FAVOR

GOD IS FAITHFUL

**worthy of belief;
loyal regardless of
another's faults or
mishaps**

*Father, I thank You for always being
a loving Father, who is always faithful
in Your love toward me.
In Jesus name. Amen.*

Psalm 100:5

For the Lord is good and his love endures forever; his faithfulness continues through all generations.

Isaiah 55:11

So is my word that goes out from my mouth: It will not return to me empty, but will accomplish what I desire and achieve the purpose for which I sent it.

I Thessalonians 5:24

The one who calls you is faithful, and he will do it.

Deuteronomy 32:4

He is the Rock, his works are perfect, and all his ways are just. A faithful God who does no wrong, upright and just is he.

Deuteronomy 7:9

Know therefore that the Lord your God is God; he is the faithful God, keeping his covenant of love to a thousand generations of those who love him and keep his commandments.

GOD IS FAITHFUL

GOD IS FAITHFUL

Psalm 40:11

Do not withhold your mercy from me,
Lord; may your love and faithfulness
always protect me.

2 Thessalonians 3:3

But the Lord is faithful, and he will
strengthen you and protect you from
the evil one.

Hebrews 10:23

Let us hold unswervingly to the hope
we profess, for he who promised is
faithful.

Isaiah 54:10

Though the mountains be shaken
and the hills be removed, yet my
unfailing love for you will not be
shaken nor my covenant of peace be
removed," says the Lord, who has
compassion on you.

Psalm 97:10

Let those who love the Lord hate
evil, for he guards the lives of his
faithful ones and delivers them from
the hand of the wicked.

1 Samuel 26:23
The Lord rewards everyone for their righteousness and faithfulness. The Lord delivered you into my hands today, but I would not lay a hand on the Lord's anointed.

Psalm 33:4
For the word of the Lord is right and true; he is faithful in all he does.

Lamentations 3:22-23
Because of the Lord's great love we are not consumed, for his compassions never fail. They are new every morning; great is your faithfulness.

1 John 1:9
If we confess our sins, he is faithful and just and will forgive us our sins and purify us from all unrighteousness.

Psalm 108:4
For great is your love, higher than the heavens; your faithfulness reaches to the skies.

GOD IS FAITHFUL

FOCUS

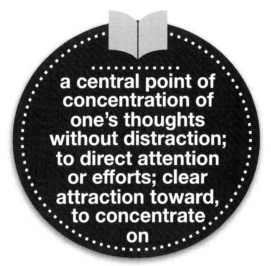

a central point of
concentration of
one's thoughts
without distraction;
to direct attention
or efforts; clear
attraction toward,
to concentrate
on

*Father God, I thank You for removing
distractions from my life and giving
me a clear, concise focus on Your
plan for me. In Jesus name.*

2 Corinthians 4:18

So we fix our eyes not on what is seen, but on what is unseen, since what is seen is temporary, but what is unseen is eternal.

Psalm 141:8

But my eyes are fixed on you, Sovereign Lord; in you I take refuge —do not give me over to death.

Hebrews 12:2

Fixing our eyes on Jesus, the pioneer and perfecter of faith. For the joy set before him he endured the cross, scorning its shame, and sat down at the right hand of the throne of God.

Proverbs 15:22

Refuse good advice and watch your plans fail; take good counsel and watch them succeed.

Proverbs 16:9

A man's heart plans his way, but the Lord directs his steps.

FOCUS

FORGIVENESS

to release an offense, treat as not guilty and to consider as if it never occurred

Father, I thank You for allowing me to walk in forgiveness and never to hold offense in my heart regardless of the offense. In Jesus name. Amen.

Matthew 6:14

For if you forgive men when they sin against you, your heavenly Father will also forgive you.

Ephesians 1:7

In him we have redemption through his blood, the forgiveness of sins, in accordance with the riches of God's grace

Colossians 3:13

Bear with each other and forgive one another if any of you has a grievance against someone. Forgive as the Lord forgave you.

Mark 11:25

And when you stand praying, if you hold anything against anyone, forgive them, so that your Father in heaven may forgive you your sins."

Luke 6:35

But love your enemies, do good to them, and lend to them without expecting anything back

FORGIVENESS

FREE FROM FEAR

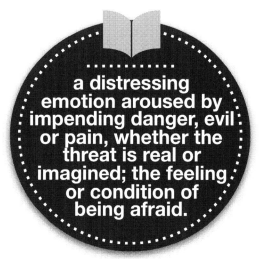

a distressing emotion aroused by impending danger, evil or pain, whether the threat is real or imagined; the feeling or condition of being afraid.

Father God, I thank You that I am totally free from fear and it no longer has any control over my life. In Jesus name. Amen.

1 John 4:18

There is no fear in love. But perfect love drives out fear, because fear has to do with punishment. The one who fears is not made perfect in love.

Psalm 23:4

Even though I walk through the darkest valley, I will fear no evil, for you are with me; your rod and your staff, they comfort me.

Psalm 112:7

They will have no fear of bad news; their hearts are steadfast, trusting in the Lord.

Isaiah 41:13

For I am the Lord, your God, who takes hold of your right hand and says to you, Do not fear; I will help you.

Isaiah 54:4

Do not be afraid; you will not suffer shame. Do not fear disgrace; you will not be humiliated.

FREE FROM FEAR

FREEDOM

the quality or state of being free; exemption from confinement, constraint or control

Father, I thank You for freeing me of every stronghold and limitation that has hindered me from walking in Your fullness. In Jesus name. Amen.

John 8:32
Then you will know the truth, and the truth will set you free."

Psalm 119:45
I will walk about in freedom, for I have sought out your precepts.

John 8:36
So if the Son sets you free, you will be free indeed.

Luke 4:18
"The Spirit of the Lord is on me, because he has anointed me to proclaim good news to the poor. He has sent me to proclaim freedom for the prisoners and recovery of sight for the blind, to set the oppressed free

2 Corinthians 3:17
Now the Lord is the Spirit, and where the Spirit of the Lord is, there is freedom.

Ephesians 3:12
In him and through faith in him we may approach God with freedom and confidence.

FREEDOM

FUTURE

existing or
occurring at a later
time or a
time to come

*Father I thank You for the glorious
plans You have for me and
for placing hope in my future.
In Jesus name. Amen.*

Jeremiah 29:11

For I know the plans I have for you," declares the Lord, "plans to prosper you and not to harm you, plans to give you hope and a future.

Psalm 37:37

Consider the blameless, observe the upright; a future awaits those who seek peace.

Job 8:7

Your beginnings will seem humble, so prosperous will your future be.

Proverbs 24:14

Know also that wisdom is like honey for you: If you find it, there is a future hope for you, and your hope will not be cut off.

Proverbs 23:18

There is surely a future hope for you, and your hope will not be cut off.

Psalm 33:11

But the plans of the Lord stand firm forever, the purposes of his heart through all generation

FUTURE

GIVING

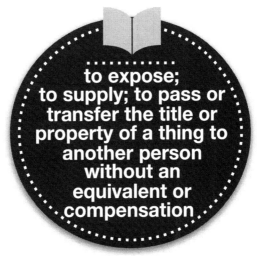

to expose;
to supply; to pass or
transfer the title or
property of a thing to
another person
without an
equivalent or
compensation

*Father, You said in Your word that
You provide seed to the sower so I
thank You for giving me the ability to
give to others. In Jesus name.*

Luke 6:38

Give, and it will be given to you. A good measure, pressed down, shaken together and running over, will be poured into your lap. For with the measure you use, it will be measured to you."

Proverbs 11:24

One person gives freely, yet gains even more; another withholds unduly, but comes to poverty.

Proverbs 18:16

A gift opens the way and ushers the giver into the presence of the great.

Deuteronomy 4:40

Keep his decrees and commands, which I am giving you today, so that it may go well with you and your children after you and that you may live long in the land the Lord your God gives you for all time.

Proverbs 22:9

The generous will themselves be blessed, for they share their food with the poor.

GIVING

GOD'S GOODNESS

acts of kindness;
favor shown;
acts of benevolence,
compassion or
mercy

*Father, You said in Your word that
Your goodness and mercy would
follow me all the days of my life
and I thank you for it.
In Jesus name. Amen.*

Psalm 27:13
I remain confident of this: I will see the goodness of the Lord in the land of the living.

Nahum 1:7
The Lord is good, a refuge in times of trouble. He cares for those who trust in him

Lamentations 3:25
The Lord is good to those whose hope is in him, to the one who seeks him;

Romans 8:28
And we know that in all things God works for the good of those who love him, who have been called according to his purpose

2 Peter 1:3
His divine power has given us everything we need for a godly life through our knowledge of him who called us by his own glory and goodness.

GOD'S GOODNESS

HEALING

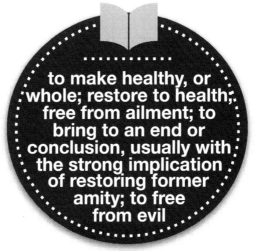

to make healthy, or whole; restore to health; free from ailment; to bring to an end or conclusion, usually with the strong implication of restoring former amity; to free from evil

Father, I thank You for bringing total and complete healing and wholeness to every broken area in my life in Jesus name.

Psalm 103:3
Who forgives all your sins and heals all your diseases,

Isaiah 53:5
But he was pierced for our trans-gressions, he was crushed for our iniquities; the punishment that brought us peace was on him, and by his wounds we are healed.

Psalm 147:3
He heals the brokenhearted and binds up their wounds.

Proverbs 12:18
The words of the reckless pierce like swords, but the tongue of the wise brings healing.

Proverbs 16:24
Gracious words are a honeycomb, sweet to the soul and healing to the bones.

Exodus 23:25
I will take away sickness from among you

HEALING

Psalm 30:2
Lord my God, I called to you for help, and you healed me.

James 5:15-16
And the prayer offered in faith will make the sick person well; the Lord will raise them up. If they have sinned, they will be forgiven. Therefore confess your sins to each other and pray for each other so that you may be healed. The prayer of a righteous person is powerful and effective.

Jeremiah 17:14
Heal me, Lord, and I will be healed; save me and I will be saved, for you are the one I praise.

Proverbs 17:22
A cheerful heart is good medicine, but a crushed spirit dries up the bones.

Proverbs 4:20-22

My son, pay attention to what I say; turn your ear to my words. Do not let them out of your sight, keep them within your heart; for they are life to those who find them and health to one's whole body.

Jeremiah 30:17

But I will restore you to health and heal your wounds, declares the Lord

Jeremiah 33:6

Nevertheless, I will bring health and healing to it; I will heal my people and will let them enjoy abundant peace and security.

Acts 10:38

How God anointed Jesus of Nazareth with the Holy Spirit and power, and how he went around doing good and healing all who were under the power of the devil, because God was with him.

HEALING

HOUSING

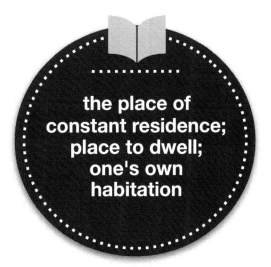

the place of
constant residence;
place to dwell;
one's own
habitation

*Father, I thank You for my own
place of residence, that is a peaceable
habitation, a safe dwelling
and a quiet resting place.
In Jesus name.*

Isaiah 32:18
My people will live in peaceful dwelling places, in secure homes, in undisturbed places of rest.

Acts 17:26
From one man he made all the nations, that they should inhabit the whole earth; and he marked out their appointed times in history and the boundaries of their lands.

Jeremiah 29:5
Build houses and settle down; plant gardens and eat what they produce.

2 Samuel 7:10
And I will provide a place for my people Israel and will plant them so that they can have a home of their own and no longer be disturbed. Wicked people will not oppress them anymore, as they did at the beginning

HOUSING

IDENTITY

the qualities or character of a person that makes them different or distinguished from others

Father, I thank You that I know who I am and who You created me to be. I totally embrace my uniqueness. In Jesus name.

Psalm 139:14

I praise you because I am fearfully and wonderfully made; your works are wonderful, I know that full well.

Genesis 1:27

So God created mankind in his own image, in the image of God he created them; male and female he created them.

Romans 8:17

Now if we are children, then we are heirs—heirs of God and co-heirs with Christ, if indeed we share in his sufferings in order that we may also share in his glory.

Galatians 2:20

I have been crucified with Christ and I no longer live, but Christ lives in me. The life I now live in the body, I live by faith in the Son of God, who loved me and gave himself for me.

Ephesians 2:10

For we are God's handiwork, created in Christ Jesus to do good works

IDENTITY

INCREASE

to make greater, as in number, size, strength, or quality; to swell or enlarge; to extend; to lengthen

*Father, I thank You increasing me
in every area of my life.
In Jesus name.
Amen.*

Genesis 1:28

God blessed them and said to them, "Be fruitful and increase in number; fill the earth and subdue it. Rule over the fish in the sea and the birds in the sky and over every living creature that moves on the ground."

Deuteronomy 1:11

May the Lord, the God of your ancestors, increase you a thousand times and bless you as he has promised!

2 Corinthians 9:10

Now he who supplies seed to the sower and bread for food will also supply and increase your store of seed and will enlarge the harvest of your righteousness.

Leviticus 26:9

I will look on you with favor and make you fruitful and increase your numbers, and I will keep my covenant with you.

INCREASE

JOY

the emotion of great delight or state of happiness caused by something exceptionally good or satisfying

Father, I thank You for engulfing my heart with unexplainable joy that strengthens my life.
In Jesus name.

James 1:2-3

Consider it pure joy, my brothers and sisters, whenever you face trials of many kinds, because you know that the testing of your faith produces perseverance.

Job 8:21

He will yet fill your mouth with laughter and your lips with shouts of joy.

Nehemiah 8:10

Nehemiah said, "Go and enjoy choice food and sweet drinks, and send some to those who have nothing prepared. This day is holy to our Lord. Do not grieve, for the joy of the Lord is your strength."

John 16:24

Until now you have not asked for anything in my name. Ask and you will receive, and your joy will be complete.

JOY

LIFE

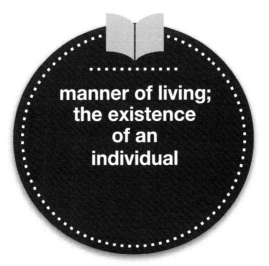

manner of living;
the existence
of an
individual

*Father, I thank You for adding great
value to my life and causing me
to have a life of greatness.
In Jesus name. Amen*

John 10:10
The thief comes only to steal and kill and destroy; I have come that they may have life, and have it to the full.

John 4:1-4
In the beginning was the Word, and the Word was with God, and the Word was God. He was with God in the beginning. Through him all things were made; without him nothing was made that has been made. In him was life, and that life was the light of all mankind.

Job 33:28
God has delivered me from going down to the pit, and I shall live to enjoy the light of life

Psalm 25:20
Guard my life and rescue me; do not let me be put to shame, for I take refuge in you.

Proverbs 22:4
Humility is the fear of the Lord; its wages are riches and honor and life.

LONG LIFE

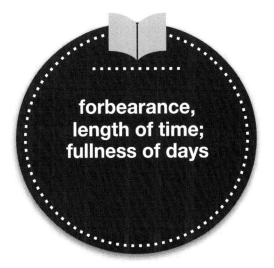

forbearance,
length of time;
fullness of days

*Father, I thank You for satisfying me
with long life and giving me the
fullness of my days.
In Jesus name. Amen*

Proverbs 3:1-2

My son, do not forget my teaching, but keep my commands in your heart, for they will prolong your life many years and bring you peace and prosperity.

1 Samuel 25:6

Say to him: 'Long life to you! Good health to you and your household! And good health to all that is yours!

Exodus 23:26

Worship the Lord your God, and his blessing will be on your food and water. I will take away sickness from among you, and none will miscarry or be barren in your land. I will give you a full life span.

Ephesians 6:2-3

"Honor your father and mother"— which is the first commandment with a promise— "so that it may go well with you and that you may enjoy long life on the earth.

LONG LIFE

Psalm 91:16

With long life I will satisfy him and show him my salvation."

Genesis 6:3

Then the Lord said, "My Spirit will not contend with humans forever, for they are mortal; their days will be a hundred and twenty years."

Proverbs 3:13-16

Blessed are those who find wisdom, those who gain understanding, for she is more profitable than silver and yields better returns than gold. She is more precious than rubies; nothing you desire can compare with her. Long life is in her right hand; in her left hand are riches and honor.

Proverbs 4:10

Listen, my son, accept what I say, and the years of your life will be many.

LONG LIFE

Deuteronomy 6:1-2

These are the commands, decrees and laws the Lord your God directed me to teach you to observe in the land that you are crossing the Jordan to possess, so that you, your children and their children after them may fear the Lord your God as long as you live by keeping all his decrees and commands that I give you, and so that you may enjoy long life.

Proverbs 9:10-11

The fear of the Lord is the beginning of wisdom, and knowledge of the Holy One is understanding. For through wisdom[a] your days will be many, and years will be added to your life.

Proverbs 10:27

The fear of the Lord adds length to life, but the years of the wicked are cut short.

LONG LIFE

MERCY

benevolence,
mildness or tenderness
of heart which
disposes a person to
overlook injuries, or to
treat an offender
better than he
deserves

*Father, I give You praise and thank
You that Your mercy for
me is new everyday.
In Jesus name. Amen.*

Exodus 33:19

And the Lord said, "I will cause all my goodness to pass in front of you, and I will proclaim my name, the Lord, in your presence. I will have mercy on whom I will have mercy, and I will have compassion on whom I will have compassion.

Isaiah 55:6-7

Seek the Lord while he may be found; call on him while he is near. Let the wicked forsake their ways and the unrighteous their thoughts. Let them turn to the Lord, and he will have mercy on them, and to our God, for he will freely pardon.

Titus 3:5

He saved us, not because of righteous things we had done, but because of his mercy. He saved us through the washing of rebirth and renewal by the Holy Spirit

James 5:11

The Lord is full of compassion and mercy.

MERCY

OBEDIENCE

compliance with a command; be in submission to authority

Father, I thank You that I have the heart to be obedient to Your word so I can receive all that You have for me. In Jesus name.

Job 36:11

If they obey and serve him, they will spend the rest of their days in prosperity and their years in contentment.

Jeremiah 7:23

But I gave them this command: Obey me, and I will be your God and you will be my people. Walk in obedience to all I command you, that it may go well with you.

Deuteronomy 5:33

Walk in obedience to all that the Lord your God has commanded you, so that you may live and prosper and prolong your days in the land that you will possess.

Deuteronomy 30:16

For I command you today to love the Lord your God, to walk in obedience to him, and to keep his commands, decrees and laws; then you will live and increase, and the Lord your God will bless you in the land you are entering to possess.

OBEDIENCE

PATIENCE

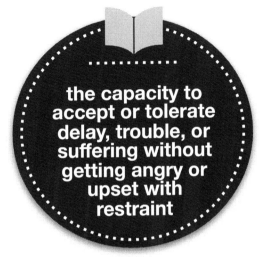

the capacity to accept or tolerate delay, trouble, or suffering without getting angry or upset with restraint

Father, I thank You for giving me patience as I seek Your perfect will for my life. In Jesus name.

Proverbs 14:29
Whoever is patient has great understanding, but one who is quick-tempered displays folly.

Psalm 40:1-2
I waited patiently for the Lord; he turned to me and heard my cry. He lifted me out of the slimy pit, out of the mud and mire; he set my feet on a rock and gave me a firm place to stand.

James 5:7-8
Be patient, then, brothers and sisters, until the Lord's coming. See how the farmer waits for the land to yield its valuable crop, patiently waiting for the autumn and spring rains. 8 You too, be patient and stand firm, because the Lord's coming is near.

Psalm 27:14
Wait for the Lord; be strong and take heart and wait for the Lord.

PATIENCE

PEACE

freedom of the mind from annoyance, distraction, or anxiety; freedom from any strife; state of mutual harmony

Father, I thank You that Your peace, which surpasses my understanding will continue to guard my heart and mind. In Jesus name. Amen.

Psalm 85:8

I will listen to what God the Lord says; he promises peace to his people, his faithful servants— but let them not turn to folly.

2 Corinthians 13:11

Finally, brothers and sisters, rejoice! Strive for full restoration, encourage one another, be of one mind, live in peace. And the God of love and peace will be with you.

Philippians 4:6-7

Do not be anxious about anything, but in every situation, by prayer and petition, with thanksgiving, present your requests to God. And the peace of God, which transcends all understanding, will guard your hearts and your minds in Christ Jesus.

Isaiah 26:3

You will keep in perfect peace those whose minds are steadfast, because they trust in you.

PEACE

PERSEVERANCE

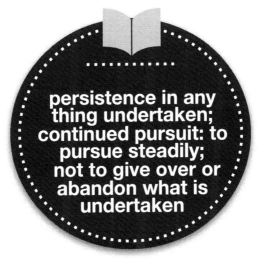

persistence in any
thing undertaken;
continued pursuit: to
pursue steadily;
not to give over or
abandon what is
undertaken

*Father, I thank You for giving me the
persistence to persevere for the
pursuit of my dreams and goals
and see them to fulfillment.
In Jesus name. Amen.*

James 1:3-4

Because you know that the testing of your faith produces perseverance. Let perseverance finish its work so that you may be mature and complete, not lacking anything.

Hebrews 12:1

Therefore, since we are surrounded by such a great cloud of witnesses, let us throw off everything that hinders and the sin that so easily entangles. And let us run with perseverance the race marked out for us

Romans 5:3-4

Not only so, but we also glory in our sufferings, because we know that suffering produces perseverance; perseverance, character; and character, hope.

Hebrews 10:36

You need to persevere so that when you have done the will of God, you will receive what he has promised.

PERSEVERANCE

PLANS

the form of something to be done existing in the mind; representation of any intended work; An intention or decision about what one is going to do

Father God, in the name of Jesus, I embrace every plan You have for my life and I believe those plans are to prosper me and never to harm me. Amen.

Proverbs 15:22
Plans fail for lack of counsel, but with many advisers they succeed.

Proverbs 16:3
Commit to the Lord whatever you do, and he will establish your plans.

Psalm 20:4
May he give you the desire of your heart and make all your plans succeed.

Jeremiah 29:11
For I know the plans I have for you," declares the Lord, "plans to prosper you and not to harm you, plans to give you hope and a future.

Proverbs 19:21
Many are the plans in a person's heart, but it is the Lord's purpose that prevails.

Proverbs 21:5
The plans of the diligent lead to profit as surely as haste leads to poverty.

PLANS

PRAYER

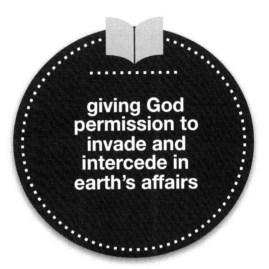

giving God permission to invade and intercede in earth's affairs

Father, I thank You for always hearing my prayers and interceding for me on my behalf. In Jesus Name. Amen.

Genesis 25:21

Isaac prayed to the Lord on behalf of his wife, because she was child-less. The Lord answered his prayer, and his wife Rebekah became pregnant.

Mark 11:24

Therefore I tell you, whatever you ask for in prayer, believe that you have received it, and it will be yours.

Psalm 143:1

Lord, hear my prayer, listen to my cry for mercy; in your faithfulness and righteousness come to my relief.

Psalm 17:6

I call on you, my God, for you will answer me; turn your ear to me and hear my prayer.

Psalm 66:20

Praise be to God, who has not rejected my prayer or withheld his love from me

Psalm 54:2

Hear my prayer, O God; listen to the words of my mouth.

PRAYER

PROTECTION

the act of protecting; defense; shelter from evil; preservation from loss, injury or annoyance

Father God, I thank You for Your hedge of protection surrounding my life like a shield.
In Jesus name. Amen.

Isaiah 54:17

No weapon forged against you will prevail, and you will refute every tongue that accuses you. This is the heritage of the servants of the Lord, and this is their vindication from me," declares the Lord.

Psalm 91:1-7

Whoever dwells in the shelter of the Most High will rest in the shadow of the Almighty. I will say of the Lord, "He is my refuge and my fortress, my God, in whom I trust." Surely he will save you from the fowler's snare and from the deadly pestilence. He will cover you with his feathers, and under his wings you will find refuge; his faithfulness will be your shield and ram-part. You will not fear the terror of night, nor the arrow that flies by day, nor the pestilence that stalks in the darkness, nor the plague that destroys at midday. A thousand may fall at your side, ten thousand at your right hand, but it will not come near you.

PROTECTION

2 Thessalonians 3:3

But the Lord is faithful, and he will strengthen you and protect you from the evil one.

Proverbs 2:7-8

He holds success in store for the upright, he is a shield to those whose walk is blameless, for he guards the course of the just and protects the way of his faithful ones.

Psalm 91:14-15

"Because he loves me," says the Lord, "I will rescue him; I will protect him, for he acknowledges my name. He will call on me, and I will answer him; I will be with him in trouble, I will deliver him and honor him.

Psalm 9:9

The Lord is a refuge for the oppressed, a stronghold in times of trouble.

Psalm 32:7

You are my hiding place; you will protect me from trouble and surround me with songs of deliverance.

Psalm 55:22

Cast your cares on the Lord and he will sustain you; he will never let the righteous be shaken.

Psalm 3:3

But you, Lord, are a shield around me, my glory, the One who lifts my head high.

Psalm 119:114

You are my refuge and my shield; I have put my hope in your word.

Psalm 18:2

The Lord is my rock, my fortress and my deliverer; my God is my rock, in whom I take refuge, my shield and the horn of my salvation, my stronghold.

PROTECTION

PROVISION OF GOD

the act of providing or making previous preparation; to procure beforehand; to get, collect or make ready for future use; to furnish or supply

Father, You said in Your word that You would supply all of my needs according to Your riches in glory by Christ Jesus and I thank You for it. In Jesus name.

Genesis 22:14

So Abraham called that place The Lord Will Provide. And to this day it is said, "On the mountain of the Lord it will be provided.

Psalm 65:9

You care for the land and water it; you enrich it abundantly. The streams of God are filled with water to provide the people with grain, for so you have ordained it.

Psalm 111:5

He provides food for those who fear him; he remembers his covenant forever.

Psalm 144:13

Our barns will be filled with every kind of provision. Our sheep will increase by thousands, by tens of thousands in our fields;

Psalm 132:15

I will bless her with abundant provisions; her poor I will satisfy with food.

PROVISION OF GOD

PURPOSE

the reason why something was birthed, born or created; an intentional design that always includes the end in view

Father, I truly thank You for revealing to me, my purpose on this earth and Your intentional design for my life. In Jesus name. Amen.

Proverbs 19:21

Many are the plans in a person's heart, but it is the Lord's purpose that prevails

Proverbs 20:5

The purposes of a person's heart are deep waters, but one who has insight draws them out.

Romans 8:28

And we know that in all things God works for the good of those who love him, who have been called according to his purpose.

Jeremiah 1:5

Before I formed you in the womb I knew you, before you were born I set you apart; I appointed you as a prophet to the nations."

Ephesians 1:11

In him we were also chosen, having been predestined according to the plan of him who works out everything in conformity with the purpose of his will

PURPOSE

REWARD

to repay, recompense, compensate or equivalent return for good done, for kindness, for services and the like

Father, I thank You for being a rewarder of those that diligently seek you. In Jesus name. Amen.

Hebrews 10:35

So do not throw away your confidence; it will be richly rewarded.

Hebrews 11:6

And without faith it is impossible to please God, because anyone who comes to him must believe that he exists and that he rewards those who earnestly seek him.

Psalm 18:24

The Lord has rewarded me according to my righteousness, according to the cleanness of my hands in his sight.

Genesis 15:1

After this, the word of the Lord came to Abram in a vision: "Do not be afraid, Abram. I am your shield, your very great reward."

Ruth 2:12

May the Lord repay you for what you have done. May you be richly rewarded by the Lord, the God of Israel, under whose wings you have come to take refuge."

REWARD

RIGHTEOUSNESS

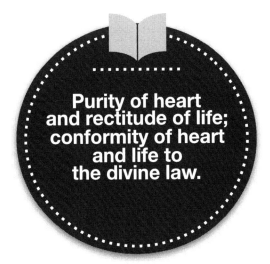

**Purity of heart
and rectitude of life;
conformity of heart
and life to
the divine law.**

*Father, I thank You that I am the
righteousness of God in Christ
Jesus, created for good works.
In Jesus name.*

Psalm 33:5
The Lord loves righteousness and justice; the earth is full of his unfailing love.

Psalm 35:28
My tongue will proclaim your righteousness, your praises all day long.

Isaiah 58:6
Then your light will break forth like the dawn, and your healing will quickly appear; then your righteousness will go before you, and the glory of the Lord will be your rear guard.

Genesis 15:6
Abram believed the Lord, and he credited it to him as righteousness

Psalm 18:24
The Lord has rewarded me according to my righteousness, according to the cleanness of my hands in his sight.

Psalm 85:13
Righteousness goes before him and prepares the way for his steps.

RIGHTEOUSNESS

SEEKING GOD

to go after; to follow; to go in search or quest of; to eagerly hunt

Father, Your word says if I seek You, I will find You and I thank You for opening up a new world of understanding to me as I seek You. In Jesus name. Amen

2 Chronicles 26:5

He sought God during the days of Zechariah, who instructed him in the fear of God. As long as he sought the Lord, God gave him success.

Psalm 34:10

The lions may grow weak and hungry, but those who seek the Lord lack no good thing.

Matthew 6:33

But seek first his kingdom and his righteousness, and all these things will be given to you as well.

Deuteronomy 4:29

But if from there you seek the Lord your God, you will find him if you seek him with all your heart and with all your soul.

Proverbs 11:27

Whoever seeks good finds favor, but evil comes to one who searches for it.

Proverbs 8:17

I love those who love me, and those who seek me find me.

SEEKING GOD

SELF-CONTROL

the virtue of one
who masters his
own emotions,
desires and
passions; the ability
to control oneself

*Father, I thank you that I possess
the fruit of self-control and I
exercise it everyday and in every way.
In Jesus name. Amen.*

Galatians 6:22,23

But the fruit of the Spirit is love, joy, peace, forbearance, kindness, goodness, faithfulness, gentleness and self-control.

Titus 2:11-12

For the grace of God has appeared that offers salvation to all people. It teaches us to say "No" to ungodliness and worldly passions, and to live self-controlled, upright and godly lives in this present age

Proverbs 16:32

Better a patient person than a warrior, one with self-control than one who takes a city

1 Peter 5:8

Be alert and of sober mind. Your enemy the devil prowls around like a roaring lion looking for someone to devour.

II Timothy 1:7

For the Spirit God gave us does not make us timid, but gives us power, love and self-discipline.

SELF-CONTROL

SOWING &
REAPING

to reap and gather
what has been
planted

*Father, I thank You for the beauty of
sowing and reaping. Every time I sow
seed, I always reap an exponential
harvest. In Jesus name. Amen.*

Luke 6:38

Give, and it will be given to you. A good measure, pressed down, shaken together and running over, will be poured into your lap. For with the measure you use, it will be measured to you

Genesis 8:22

"As long as the earth endures, seed-time and harvest, cold and heat, summer and winter, day and night will never cease."

2 Corinthians 9:6

Remember this: whoever sows sparingly will also reap sparingly, and whoever sows generously will also reap generously.

Psalm 126:5

Those who sow with tears will reap with songs of joy.

Proverbs 11:18

A wicked person earns deceptive wages, but the one who sows righteousness reaps a sure reward.

SOWING AND REAPING

STABILITY

firmness; strength to stand without being moved or overthrown

Father, I thank You for causing me to have stability in my mind, emotions and in my actions. In Jesus name. Amen.

Luke 6:48

They are like a man building a house, who dug down deep and laid the foundation on rock. When a flood came, the torrent struck that house but could not shake it, because it was well built.

Psalm 62:1-2

Truly my soul finds rest in God; my salvation comes from him. Truly he is my rock and my salvation; he is my fortress, I will never be shaken.

Psalm 37:23-24

The Lord makes firm the steps of the one who delights in him; though he may stumble, he will not fall, for the Lord upholds him with his hand.

1 Corinthians 15:58

Therefore, my dear brothers and sisters, stand firm. Let nothing move you. Always give yourselves fully to the work of the Lord, because you know that your labor in the Lord is not in vain.

STABILITY

STRENGTH

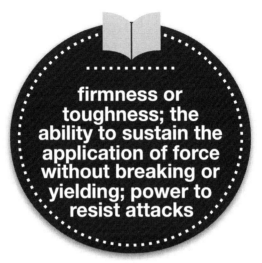

firmness or toughness; the ability to sustain the application of force without breaking or yielding; power to resist attacks

Father, I thank You that whatever I've faced in my life, You always infuse me with Your inner strength. In Jesus name. Amen.

Isaiah 40:29

He gives strength to the weary and increases the power of the weak.

Psalm 28:7

The Lord is my strength and my shield; my heart trusts in him, and he helps me. My heart leaps for joy, and with my song I praise him.

Ephesians 3:16

I pray that out of his glorious riches he may strengthen you with power through his Spirit in your inner being

Philippians 4:13

I can do all this through him who gives me strength.

2 Samuel 22:33-34

It is God who arms me with strength and keeps my way secure. He makes my feet like the feet of a deer; he causes me to stand on the heights.

Isaiah 41:10

So do not fear, for I am with you; do not be dismayed, for I am your God. I will strengthen you and help you; I will uphold you with my righteous right hand

STRENGTH

SUCCESS IN BUSINESS

the favorable or prosperous determination of attempts or endeavors; the accomplishment of one's goals

Father, I thank You for always causing me to thrive in business and for blessing the work of my hands. In Jesus name. Amen.

Joshua 1:8
Keep this Book of the Law always on your lips; meditate on it day and night, so that you may be careful to do everything written in it. Then you will be prosperous and successful.

Proverbs 22:29
Do you see someone skilled in their work? They will serve before kings; they will not serve before officials of low rank.

Deuteronomy 8:18
But remember the Lord your God, for it is he who gives you the ability to produce wealth

Deuteronomy 28:8
The Lord will send a blessing on your barns and on everything you put your hand to. The Lord your God will bless you in the land he is giving you.

Proverbs 10:4
Lazy hands make for poverty, but diligent hands bring wealth.

SUCCESS IN BUSINESS

THANKFULNESS

appreciation;
an expression of
gratitude of
God's favor
on your life

Father, I thank You for giving me a
thankful heart for everything
and in everything.
In Jesus name. Amen.

Colossians 2:7

Rooted and built up in him, strengthened in the faith as you were taught, and overflowing with thankfulness.

Colossians 3:15

Let the peace of Christ rule in your hearts, since as members of one body you were called to peace. And be thankful.

Isaiah 51:3

The Lord will surely comfort Zion and will look with compassion on all her ruins; he will make her deserts like Eden, her wastelands like the garden of the Lord. Joy and gladness will be found in her, thanksgiving and the sound of singing.

Psalm 107:8-9

Let them give thanks to the Lord for his unfailing love and his wonderful deeds for mankind, for he satisfies the thirsty and fills the hungry with good things.

THANKFULNESS

THOUGHTS

something framed by the imagination; design; the workings of conscience

Father, I thank You for giving me the mind and thoughts of Christ. In Jesus name. Amen.

2 Corinthians 10:5

We demolish arguments and every pretension that sets itself up against the knowledge of God, and we take captive every thought to make it obedient to Christ.

Ephesians 3:20

Now to him who is able to do immeasurably more than all we ask or imagine, according to his power that is at work within us

Philippians 2:5

In your relationships with one another, have the same mindset as Christ Jesus

Romans 12:2

Do not conform to the pattern of this world, but be transformed by the renewing of your mind. Then you will be able to test and approve what God's will is—his good, pleasing and perfect will.

Romans 8:6

But the mind governed by the Spirit is life and peace.

THOUGHTS

IN TIMES OF TROUBLE

to disturb the mental calm and contentment of; worry, distress or agitation; to put to inconvenience

Father, I thank You for being with me in times of trouble and always leading and guiding me through. In Jesus name. Amen.

Psalm 20:1

May the Lord answer you when you are in distress; may the name of the God of Jacob protect you.

John 16:33

"I have told you these things, so that in me you may have peace. In this world you will have trouble. But take heart! I have overcome the world."

Psalm 46:1

God is our refuge and strength, an ever-present help in trouble.

Psalm 25:17

Relieve the troubles of my heart and free me from my anguish.

Psalm 32:7

You are my hiding place; you will protect me from trouble and surround me with songs of deliverance.

Psalm 34:19

The righteous person may have many troubles, but the Lord delivers him from them all

TRUST

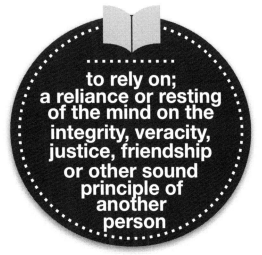

to rely on;
a reliance or resting
of the mind on the
integrity, veracity,
justice, friendship
or other sound
principle of
another
person

*Father, I thank You that my total
trust and reliance is on You in
everything I do.
In Jesus name. Amen.*

Proverbs 3:5-6

Trust in the Lord with all your heart and lean not on your own understanding; in all your ways submit to him, and he will make your paths straight.

Titus 3:8

This is a trustworthy saying. And I want you to stress these things, so that those who have trusted in God may be careful to devote themselves to doing what is good. These things are excellent and profitable for everyone.

Jeremiah 17:7-8

But blessed is the one who trusts in the Lord, whose confidence is in him. They will be like a tree planted by the water that sends out its roots by the stream. It does not fear when heat comes; its leaves are always green. It has no worries in a year of drought and never fails to bear fruit."

Psalm 25:1

In you, Lord my God, I put my trust.

TRUST

UNDERSTANDING

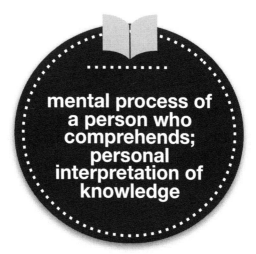

mental process of
a person who
comprehends;
personal
interpretation of
knowledge

*Father, I thank You that in all my
getting, I get an understanding of
Your will, plan and purpose for my
life. In Jesus name. Amen.*

Philippians 4:7
And the peace of God, which transcends all understanding, will guard your hearts and your minds in Christ Jesus

Proverbs 2:11
Discretion will protect you, and understanding will guard you.

Proverbs 3:13
Blessed are those who find wisdom, those who gain understanding,

Exodus 31:3
And I have filled him with the Spirit of God, with wisdom, with understanding, with knowledge and with all kinds of skills

Proverbs 3:5
Trust in the Lord with all your heart and lean not on your own understanding

Proverbs 4:7
The beginning of wisdom is this: Get wisdom. Though it cost all you have, get understanding.

UNDERSTANDING

UNITY

the state of being one; oneness of mind; agreement; uniformity

Father, I thank You for causing me to become one with Your word, so that I may see Your word manifest in my life. In Jesus name. Amen.

Psalm 133:1
How good and pleasant it is when God's people live together in unity!

Ephesians 4:3
Make every effort to keep the unity of the Spirit through the bond of peace.

John 17:23
I in them and you in me—so that they may be brought to complete unity. Then the world will know that you sent me and have loved them even as you have loved me.

Psalm 133:1
How good and pleasant it is when God's people live together in unity!

Ephesians 4:13
Until we all reach unity in the faith and in the knowledge of the Son of God and become mature, attaining to the whole measure of the fullness of Christ.

UNITY

VICTORY

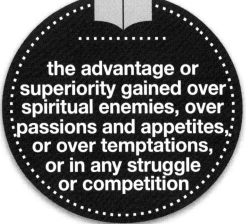

the advantage or superiority gained over spiritual enemies, over passions and appetites, or over temptations, or in any struggle or competition

Father, I thank You that Jesus has already defeated every adversary and won the victory for me. I also thank you that I experience "sweatless victories" daily. In Jesus name. Amen

1 Corinthians 15:57
But thanks be to God! He gives us the victory through our Lord Jesus Christ.

1 John 5:4
For everyone born of God overcomes the world. This is the victory that has overcome the world, even our faith.

Proverbs 24:6
Surely you need guidance to wage war, and victory is won through many advisers.

Deuteronomy 20:4
For the Lord your God is the one who goes with you to fight for you against your enemies to give you victory.

Psalm 20:6
Now this I know: The Lord gives victory to his anointed. He answers him from his heavenly sanctuary with the victorious power of his right hand.

Psalm 44:7
But you give us victory over our enemies, you put our adversaries to shame.

VICTORY

John 16:33

"I have told you these things, so that in me you may have peace. In this world you will have trouble. But take heart! I have overcome the world."

2 Corinthians 2:14

But thanks be to God, who always leads us as captives in Christ's triumphal procession and uses us to spread the aroma of the knowledge of him everywhere.

Psalm 20:6-9

Now this I know: The Lord gives victory to his anointed. He answers him from his heavenly sanctuary with the victorious power of his right hand. Some trust in chariots and some in horses, but we trust in the name of the Lord our God. They are brought to their knees and fall, but we rise up and stand firm. Lord, give victory to the king! Answer us when we call!

VICTORY

Romans 8:37
No, in all these things we are more than conquerors through him who loved us.

Proverbs 16:7
When the Lord takes pleasure in anyone's way, he causes their enemies to make peace with them.

Romans 8:31
What, then, shall we say in response to these things? If God is for us, who can be against us?

1 John 4:4
You, dear children, are from God and have overcome them, because the one who is in you is greater than the one who is in the world.

Revelation 12:11
They triumphed over him by the blood of the Lamb and by the word of their testimony;

VICTORY

WILL OF GOD

God's desires, plans and purposes for His children's lives

Father, I thank You that Your perfect will for my life is being made known to me. In Jesus name. Amen.

1 Thessalonians 4:3-5

It is God's will that you should be sanctified: that you should avoid sexual immorality; that each of you should learn to control your own body in a way that is holy and honorable, not in passionate lust like the pagans, who do not know God;

1 Thessalonians 5:18

Give thanks in all circumstances; for this is God's will for you in Christ Jesus

1 John 2:17

The world and its desires pass away, but whoever does the will of God lives forever.

Ephesians 1:11-12

In him we were also chosen, having been predestined according to the plan of him who works out everything in conformity with the purpose of his will, in order that we, who were the first to put our hope in Christ, might be for the praise of his glory.

WILL OF GOD

WISDOM

the quality or state
of being wise;
discernment

*Father, I thank You that I walk in
superior wisdom concerning every
area of my life. In Jesus name.
Amen.*

James 1:5
If any of you lacks wisdom, you should ask God, who gives generously to all without finding fault, and it will be given to you.

1 Corinthians 1:30
It is because of him that you are in Christ Jesus, who has become for us wisdom from God—that is, our righteousness, holiness and redemption.

Proverbs 4:7
The beginning of wisdom is this: Get wisdom. Though it cost all you have, get understanding.

Psalm 111:10
The fear of the Lord is the beginning of wisdom; all who follow his precepts have good understanding. To him belongs eternal praise.

Ecclesiastes 7:19
Wisdom makes one wise person more powerful than ten rulers in a city.

WISDOM

Proverbs 16:16
How much better to get wisdom than gold, to get insight rather than silver!

Proverbs 24:14
Know also that wisdom is like honey for you: If you find it, there is a future hope for you, and your hope will not be cut off.

Ecclesiastes 7:11-12
Wisdom, like an inheritance, is a good thing and benefits those who see the sun. Wisdom is a shelter as money is a shelter, but the advantage of knowledge is this: Wisdom preserves those who have it.

1 Corinthians 1:25
For the foolishness of God is wiser than human wisdom, and the weakness of God is stronger than human strength.

Psalm 90:12
Teach us to number our days, that we may gain a heart of wisdom.

Proverbs 2:6
For the Lord gives wisdom; from his mouth come knowledge and understanding.

Proverbs 2:12
Wisdom will save you from the ways of wicked men, from men whose words are perverse,

Proverbs 4:6
Do not forsake wisdom, and she will protect you; love her, and she will watch over you.

Proverbs 19:8
The one who gets wisdom loves life; the one who cherishes understanding will soon prosper.

Proverbs 28:26
Those who trust in themselves are fools, but those who walk in wisdom are kept safe.

WISDOM

WORK

to act; to carry on operations; to be in action or motion; to produce by action; to labor; to carry out business

Father, I thank You for always blessing the work of my hands.
In Jesus name.
Amen.

Colossians 3:23
Whatever you do, work at it with all your heart, as working for the Lord, not for human masters

Genesis 2:15
The Lord God took the man and put him in the Garden of Eden to work it and take care of it.

Proverbs 14:23
All hard work brings a profit, but mere talk leads only to poverty.

Proverbs 10:4
Lazy hands make for poverty, but diligent hands bring wealth.

Titus 3:14
Our people must learn to devote themselves to doing what is good, in order to provide for urgent needs and not live unproductive lives.

1 Corinthians 15:58
Let nothing move you. Always give yourselves fully to the work of the Lord, because you know that your labor in the Lord is not in vain.

WORK

Daily Affirmation:
Speak this over your life every day!

- I lean on God for being my provider
- I know how to encourage myself and I don't wait for someone else to tell me who I am or how great I am
- I am a wonder-filled man, a great husband, protector, and a awesome provider
- I keep myself in the best condition possible
- I was born to excel at everything I do
- I have eyes for my wife and only her
- I spend one on one time with each of my children so that I may build a productive relationship with each of them, pour into them and nurture their gifting
- I choose to speak life and point out the good in those around me
- I know how to go to God and receive the answers I need
- I don't waste time watching others build their empire but I spend time daily working on my dreams so that I can build my own empire therefore enabling me leave a legacy for my children's children
- I use the gifts God gave me to start businesses and be the solution to someone else's problem
- I look for innovative ways to generate new business

- I use my God-given talents and abilities in the marketplace and it causes wealth to be attracted to me through multiple streams of income
- My ultimate goal is to have a highly successful business even if I'm working at a job
- I am a good steward over my possessions and am financially saavy & intelligent
- My financial intelligence causes me to be a earn, save, sow, spend and invest wisely
- I am a man driven by purpose and integrity
- My eyes are open to the things God needs me to be alert to and aware of
- I talk to God on a daily basis concerning my inner most frustrations and weights that I carry as a man
- I love myself and won't ever allow the pain of the past to creep back into my future
- I live by faith and was born to do great things
- I don't allow distractions to over take me because I'm highly focused on my dreams and my goals.
- My focus is my purpose and the plan God has for me
- I am a winner, a champion, I'm powerful, victorious and full of faith
- I trust God in every area of my life.

Have You Accepted Jesus Christ As Your Lord & Savior?

The Bible says, "That if you confess with your mouth the Lord Jesus and believe in your heart that God raised Him from the dead, you will be saved." Romans 10:9

If you just believe in your heart that the same resurrection power that God used to raise Jesus Christ from the dead can resurrect you from whatever dead state that you are in, then the Word of God says, "You will be saved."

Pray this prayer from your heart today!

Father, I confess Jesus Christ as Lord over my life right now. I believe in my heart that You raised Jesus from the dead. God, I ask you to forgive me of all my sins. Lord, I thank you for saving me. In Jesus Name, Amen.